A Fire Without Light

Darren C. Demaree

Nixes Mate Books
Allston, Massachusetts

Copyright © 2017 Darren C. Demaree

Book design by d'Entremont
Cover photograph from the collection of Lauren Leja

All rights reserved. This book or any portion thereof may not be reproduced or used in any manner whatsoever without the express written permission of the publisher except for the use of brief quotations in a book review or scholarly journal.

This book is dedicated to every person that believes empathy is our most important strength, and that those that believe it to be a weakness are the weakest among us. Those people that rally against love and acceptance we will remember, but we will never raise their names in song without the anger they forced into our hearts.

ISBN 978-0-9993971-5-2

Nixes Mate Books
POBox 1179
Allston, MA 02134
nixesmate.pub/books

"But, in the Trump aftermath, I've measured the costs

And benefits of loving those who don't love
Strangers. After all, I'm often the odd one –

The strangest stranger – in any field or room.
"He was weird" will be carved into my tomb."

– Sherman Alexie

"We are linked. We are not ranked. And this is a day that will change us forever because we are together. Each of us individually and collectively will never be the same again. When we elect a possible president we too often go home. We've elected an impossible president, we're never going home. We're staying together. And we're taking over."

– Gloria Steinem

"Donald Trump is worse than any horror story I've written."

– Stephen King

A Fire Without Light

A Fire Without Light #3

I like the blue. I liked that irrational hot that could take me. All this useless red, cloaked in smoke, and most of it unashamed to speak through the coughing, it's terrifying. I like song. I will get used to these short songs. I will learn what I need to do. I won't waste a single breath. I will sing as often as I can.

A Fire Without Light #4

Imagine the outcome is camps. Imagine the outcome is walls around those camps. Imagine the outcome is love shredded by barbwire around those camps. Imagine a fire without light consuming all of us that do not see the light and cannot lie about seeing the light. Imagine I could escape. Imagine I choose to not to. I know what happens in a world like this. I did not think I would have to stop imagining it.

A Fire Without Light #5

I know there are houses in the woods, but it's those houses that are not safe anymore. The voices you hear rising above the flaming spires, they are the neighbors that don't want to be neighbors. They want your name. They want to know why you make love to your wife on Sunday. They want you to put a sign above your garden that says garden, and they have questions about why you crawl under such smoke.

A Fire Without Light #10

Blunt limbs, refusing to bloom, refusing to be kissed by the wind, you hold no webbing to catch my heart. I see you bat at the air. I see you connected to the trunk wrongly. I see no birds landing on you. I see so many squirrels jumping into the fire when they run out of branch. I'll never forget that smell. I'll never forget how that smell did nothing to slow you down.

A Fire Without Light #11

I can hear only his scavenger's song. He will take all of the loose bits for himself. If he heads towards actual flesh, we will own his ass.

A Fire Without Light #12

New sorrow, old accuracy, we all arrived outside the community center to say his name with out teeth, to let bounce it around our mouths, to have it be chewed up while it left that cave, to see it injured in the world before it was ever heard by another soul. Such a chaotic thing, his name, such a weight, a violence in image and repetition, and now we're forced to taste it. Nobody wants to taste his name, but we must if we're going to mangle it properly.

A Fire Without Light #13

This is all conflict. I have no interest in a compromise. That orange snapdragon wants my children. He can't have them. That orange snapdragon wants my brothers and sisters. He can't have them. This is all conflict. This is our conflict. We will have to remove the tongues from every flower. There can be no peace while the garden is trying to taste us.

A Fire Without Light #14

Time and much of the handling of time has stopped at this crossroads. Do these years need their own name? Does the crowd in the courtyard want cake? Will we trust a single intimacy while we live in the Midwest? I am expanding my intimacy. I want my bed to spill over into the neighbor's yard. Maybe if I can give Ohio a proper show they will remember their own bodies, and stop talking about all of the women they've never touched. Will one look at my naked wife remind them that her body is not theirs?

A Fire Without Light #15

How the gold flops from the weight of gold, and how the gold becomes both things in the mirror of gold. I think we can just distract the son-of-a-bitch with some shiny shit. We can do that for four years. We could buy him. Why don't we just pay the man? That's what he wants.

A Fire Without Light #22

Let me put it another way. We're imagining hope. We're imagining Ohio. We're forced into belief. We only see the threats, the tension, and the titles of his lists.

A Fire Without Light #23

We don't need more light. We need to breathe. We need our leaders to not be dragons. Wrong. We're all dragons now. We need to learn what to do with all this fire. We need to secure the safe places.

A Fire Without Light #24

Strained faces and clutching each other, how awful all of these holiday cards will be this year. Look into the blackened corner, the creeping soot has an eye for mother and father sees it. Look into the blank fireplace. How is this happening? At least the children are smiling. They believe every rustle to be that of Santa Clause. Their only worry is that all of the doors are locked at night now, and what if there is no backup plan?

A Fire Without Light #30

If he was a stranger this would make sense, but we know all of his names. We know all of his moves. We know he waited for the darkness, so that he might be the light. We know he is not the light. We know he hates almost all of us. We know he doesn't want to lead us. We know he wants suppress us. We know he means to consume the world. We offered him the world. We know he means to consume the world. We offered him the world. We know he means to consume the world. We offered him the world.

A Fire Without Light #35

We can live in a blood house, but we have to talk about the amount of blood.

A Fire Without Light #36

The ocean has removed the tide. Did the animals, with their impeccable knowledge of the nature of the world, decide unilaterally to not deliver another beast to the hunter? He must be running low of flesh, because today I felt the first shot graze my neck. All I did was point out that his darkness was the darkest I've ever seen. All I did was say all three of his names in order and explain what each one meant to a world that didn't understand how tenuous things were becoming.

A Fire Without Light #40

Timelessness isn't a thing. Everything ends. Even the memory of the end will be lost almost immediately. What we hold is a small burning. The hope is that there is enough light to see each other's faces through the heat, the smoke, and the vernacular of the elements. I don't see anyone right now, but that doesn't mean this moment is over. That isn't what it means at all.

A Fire Without Light #41

I didn't have it in me, to seal my mouth like Berryman suggested, keeping the air of my anger inside, and dancing so little that I might be mistaken for a fearful American. I am not afraid. I'm quiet. There is no list making in my heart. I'm writing these poems all of the time, and I'm smiling while I pile them behind every Ohioan that voted for Trump. I won't have to push them over this horse-high collection. They will turn naturally, and have to swim through the thousands of pages. Most of them will give up, and turn back to my stillness. They will hold me. We will never talk about why. We will know, but we'll never have to talk about it.

A Fire Without Light #42

The meat is selfless. The vegetables are selfless. It's the tempestuous bread that needs so much care. It's the slant of his hair that needs so much care. It's the six angles of his own paunch that's dragging us towards the remarkable roulette wheel of this country's future. There is so much red. There is so much green. I know the game. Why is everything so dark while we play it?

A Fire Without Light #45

I'm not sleeping much. I'm holding my children lightly. I think my wife is catching on that my six torrents have left the riverbed. I was three people this morning. All of them are breathing, and that is the important part. I don't know which of me will survive these four years. I've quit gambling. I'm holding my children lightly just in case my strength comes back. My fists are so lovely and pink.

A Fire Without Light #52

The past was drunk. The future is drunk already. Do you really thing we're sober right now? This sort of dancing should have been a clue. The decision-makers don't even know what music is. They celebrate the silence. We cannot allow them to celebrate.

A Fire Without Light #66

Thanksgiving is in two days, and I don't want to talk to anybody. I have rehearsed the nine things I'm willing to say. Thank you for the pie. I'd love some more coffee. Could you turn up the game? Yes. No. No. I'm having a little trouble breathing. I'll go warm up the car. Thank you.

A Fire Without Light #76

The sweat of hate makes us all think we need to be rewritten into elegy. It would be better, I think, to be nothing at all than to remove the integral pieces of the few. Humanity for all. Humanity for all. Humanity for Donald J. Trump. May he find humanity before we are forced to rest against the zero.

A Fire Without Light #77

We don't need the plates. We just need the food. If we give him our plates, will he still let us eat?

A Fire Without Light #78

I've seen all of his horses march in his hand. What do you think he does with those tiny bones when he loosens his grip? He isn't an actual giant, and this isn't a fairy tale. I can't help but think he is gentle with them once he's taken their lives away. I don't think he gnaws on bones. I think he is the kid who grew way too fast, and those in charge of raising him have no idea what he's capable of doing from day to day. He breaks a bed. He gets a new bed. He rips a shirt. He gets a new shirt. He gets America. He plays with America. He spins us on his fingertips. We have no idea what happens next.

A Fire Without Light #86

I know most of Ohio wants him to make the world like most of Ohio, but I'm telling you that most of Ohio is dead. There are dead men still running on anger and racism. There are dead women kept on budgets by those angry and fearful men. We have universities, but nobody thinks about islands when they live in a land without tides. I have a dozen relatives that consider Trump a fever dream of a president. This is the first time any of them have experienced a real high. They're not handling it well. They keep threatening me. I'm not handling it well. I've been sober long enough I could help them, but I'm not there yet. I want them to have to carry this time in their lives. I want them to realize they're going to have to lie to their grandchildren about it.

A Fire Without Light #101

I'm willing to call him the sun (he'll never be the sun), if he's willing to let Sandra Cisneros make all of his decisions. She'd have him resign, but before all of that she would make him sell pumpkins in the desert for a year. She'd make him be charitable. She'd dress him in a black-laced bra, and pose for a calendar that benefits the LGTB community. Basically, I've been drowning in these Trump poems, and I wanted to think about Sandra Cisneros for an hour, so I put her in charge of Donald Trump in my mind. It was the loveliest hour I've had in a while.

A Fire Without Light #102

Think of the white bear skin he owns. Think of how awkward it must have been the first time he lay down naked on top of it. Think of how his belly would reach further down than he wanted it to, how he would see all of himself before the faceless woman entered the room, how in that one moment before she started in on him for some unknown reason (money) he would doubt the whole of the world. The man isn't stupid. He cares about what we think of him. He's had those moments where he wants to, if only one second, not be him. It's doesn't excuse anything he's done. It doesn't excuse anything he's done. It doesn't excuse anything he's done. Most of us don't think to ruin the world because we're aging terribly. Most of us are thankful for the woman. Most of us can rein in the self-doubt enough to not sacrifice the bodies of others in our name. This really is some old-school inept King bullshit.

A Fire Without Light #105

Now, we vanish those that are not moving into the street. The public displays makes sure that your name will be read once they have to deal with the weight of your whole body. Now, we vanish those that are not moving into the street. We can halve our families, and still have enough family to identify us. It only takes one voice quietly saying your name over and over again to be remembered. Now, we vanish those that are not moving into the street. I can be the one to say your name forever. I can read many names aloud in the morning of every day. I can do that. I will do that. Now, we vanish those that are not moving into the street. I can promise I won't remember the faces I don't see next to me on this street. I can promise that it doesn't matter who you were before this gathering took place.

A Fire Without Light #106

It's a frenzy, which does not mean one of us must be eaten, and does not mean that either of us needs to shut up. It means that this is an action game now, old man, and I don't take days off. You are wealthy and strong, but I am poor and stronger. I have no name to lose anyway, so when it crosses your lips in distaste, what will that mean about you? I'm already planning a celebration for when you relent.

A Fire Without Light #108

Just sit at the table and give in to all of your fear. You don't need a pistol to do the right thing, just stand up and walk away. You don't need our forgiveness. You just need to step away quickly and quietly before the houses you've stepped on are rebuilt. Those people will come for you if you're still there.

A Fire Without Light #109

These barking days don't end. The field is waiting for the display to leave the field, so it can once again be about the crop. He's threatening the ingredients of the blossom. We're marching every week. We're protesting every day. I'm averaging a poem every six hours. I'm trying to stay strong in between poems. I ate once yesterday. I haven't showered in four days. You wanted elegance?

A Fire Without Light #110

What's next might not involve me, but I have children. I'm not moving on until these hip-booted racists have lost their footing in the deep river. I'm not moving on until we can chart the history of their failures. I want lush details chronicling the reasons why we no longer listen to people like that. Once I read all of that I will go back to writing poems about my wife.

A Fire Without Light #111

I don't think there's a bone in his jaw. Let's put our thumbs two inches to the right of his chin and see how long he remains our President. Discomfort is close enough to pain for him that he won't make it very long.

A Fire Without Light #113

He's in his gold bathtub right now. He has ships and planes in there. All of the planes are crashing into all of the ships. The bathroom floor is disgusting with his play. He hasn't named a single pilot or sailor. There's no plot in this story. It's the giant narrative. How could we ever prosecute him for how he behaves beneath the clouds? There was always going to be this amount of sadness and fear when we tapped a child with too many toys to focus on the needs of others. Some of us are going to get snapped in half in his hands, and it won't even be his fault.

A Fire Without Light #115

The word can curdle if you keep it in your mouth all of the time, if you only use the angry corners of it a bit at a time. These men in their terrible and expensive suits, they're not chewing on their own tongues, they're chewing on the word. They roll it around. They play with it. They use it the same way they use motels. When there is a good enough excuse to fuck the scene they spit it on the floor, and those that adore them see the garden unfold in that bad carpet. All I see is their fat cheeks. All I see is a partial blessing of spittle. All I can think about is that it will be up to my children to clean those floors. How will they think of us while they demolish most of what it is we've built?

A Fire Without Light #116

New flowers never grow in a President's hand. They lose them while they tend to each, single afternoon of our nation. What will he do without a single petal to begin with? When he swears an oath is there any doubt he will do so with no intention of sacrificing a single atom? We don't need these men or women to be gardens, but we need to know that they understand the process of the roots, of the sunlight, of the bloom.

A Fire Without Light #117

Dried and drained, I look the same way a creek bed looks during a drought. There is no life once the mud is gone. Winter after a drought does terrible things to a person. When this is all done I will look like I've lived through a Trump presidency. It will be worth it, but damn I used to look so strong in the first days of Ohio's fall. I used to, on certain days, be a little pretty. That part of me became so useless so quickly.

A Fire Without Light #122

The eels have found the sand. They're not slowing down. They must plan on drowning in our throats. We were right to use our bodies as a fortress. I wish they had found a better way to sanctify their efforts. They wanted prayers. They got chants. They wanted God. They got to join the processional. There is no darkness that will not be met with an absolute resistance.

A Fire Without Light #127

The jelly blood is art. The real blood is art. It's how he's eating all of it that sickens me. I have lowered my spoons to watch. I've bought knives. I'm no longer hungry, but I'm grinding my teeth enough to fool my stomach. The air works though both of us, but it always makes him look like a dragon.

A Fire Without Light #128

I know the worth of a cello. I wanted to say that out loud. It feels good to remind the world of the cello. There are so many dark pearls of the art world. Let us not forget the cello! The cello is certainly an ally in this fight.

A Fire Without Light #129

The torture will be the torture. There will be torture. Close, soul-touching torture. The removal of layers of self kind of torture. Hiding. Lost coast torture. Public molestings of our humanity torture. Do not forget one incident. We will place each moment on his chest. Some of us are going to have to rise above it, to ensure the cycle ends with him. Please don't ask me to be one of those people.

A Fire Without Light #140

I spent a night refusing my bed, refusing to calm down, refusing to be taken deeper into the dark of that night, and refusing to be softened into a gold that could be melded into his crown. I woke up sleeping dogs so they could follow me as I stomped around the ravine. I woke up children so they could eat pancakes with me at 4am. I left my wife asleep, because she'd already stayed up talking to me until after midnight. I called my father and let it ring until, dazed, he picked up the phone. I told him I wasn't a feather. I told him he was a feather on the wing of a doomed bird. He told me he loved me, and then he hung up. I spent a morning crawling around on the roof of my house. All of the people I loved were safe beneath me, but I needed the whole of winter at that point. I needed to be blanketed in snow, and when I was I could finally sleep. When my neighbors came to their cars to head to work, they shook their heads at me, and I, their collective "Ugh", welcomed the judgment. I am not right to do things such as this, but I can think of no other role for me. I am too afraid the warmth is one of his tricks, and I am too afraid to spend even one whole minute silent on the issue.

A Fire Without Light #172

I am unwilling to be the good man my wife says I am. I want to overreact. I am already wounded by Ohio. I am already memorizing the names of the dead. I am against this sickness, and my relatives want to argue about the name of the virus? Being still used to be radical. Prostration acts used to be my protesting act against the selfish tides of America, but now that they are hunting us I can't lower my head. I am not safe amidst my greatest love. Somebody keeps putting bullet casings on my back porch. The note says they will be aiming for the swollen heart tattoo on my left shoulder. Will they realize it's the outline of our home once they see the skin pull pack from the poem in the middle of it?

A Fire Without Light #173

I don't believe a soul can come out of nothing, and he has yet to show me anything more than a heaving meat-suit.

A Fire Without Light #174

The village is quiet. The cities are on fire. The forests are almost gone. Once we can see each other from any distance, the world will swallow itself.

A Fire Without Light #193

We know the cut, but we don't yet know the scar. We were never pretty, but this, this one is going to be an identifying mark. This will be what the world remembers about us for a long time.

A Fire Without Light #226

Demolish the idea of the floating cities. This was a dust world and can be a dust world again. After we eat the gigantic veil of Trump, we will need to spend the next decades in the fields and in the gardens. The forests will save us again, but we must make an offering to the dirt. The dirt must be the darkest thing in our world. Remove the cold smoke. Key the light. Shove your wrists into the deepest sparkle, and let it make you dark and dirty in the revolution of our world.

A Fire Without Light #244

The blush grows like a bloom, but it's not a bloom. The rise to the face only is a flag for the rest of the world to doubt. If we moved like we would never get old, then we would never get old. This country is orange-faced and confused by how much it hates the pole we keep promising to shove up it. Most of these things are as made up as the gods.

A Fire Without Light #245

I've hollowed out my kitchen floor. If we need to hide the body it's ready. If we need to hide my neighbors from whatever new police is coming it's ready. If it looks like I'm not home, I am in the floor in the kitchen, working on some of my own anger. I'm always home. I'm always writing these poems. I have no interest in any other battles.

A Fire Without Light #246

How many mouths did he think would stay open once he had nothing else to offer us?

A Fire Without Light #252

This ends with the smallest, strongest woman I know cornering him to growl the words she must invent. One finger directed at his face, and the cutting syllables of a woman that has no other choice. That could end any of us. It's his turn. There's a line developing all the way through America. It's so beautiful, this terrific anger they're holding on to, and every day I fall in love with every one of their clenched fists.

A Fire Without Light #325

Bark and saw, I read the phrase "peaceful ethnic cleansing" today, and I lost my posture for a second. I crawled into my own heart and I died for a second. I went into the basement to look at all of my own secrets that I always manage to metaphor into something awake yet still hidden, and I pulled them down around me. I stood up on the unfinished floor, and I felt my muscles tighten against the air of the idea of any cleansing. I kicked at my own mess a bit. Some men, some ideas of men, should be buried at sea while they're still living. I cannot advocate any violence, but at a certain point wouldn't it be self-defense? I had to remove whole parts of my person to live in the world I wanted to, and I suppose that was a needed violence I took part in. I am alive as a partial person. I am better as a partial person. I suppose some people are lost completely, and cannot be saved.

A Fire Without Light #340

The ocean is full of motherfuckers that believed they were the ocean.

A Fire Without Light #341

Winter beneath my shirt, my nipples have become very political, and the one on the right has refused to acknowledge that winter is here. The wind howls and the fabric I've chosen is enough for my right nipple? How could one body swallow a season so completely, and have one nob in one quadrant maintain that this is the summer we've been waiting for? I have no desire to lose my own nipple. I am going to cut a hole in my all of my shirts to see how long the right can take this new discomfort the rest of the world is experiencing. I refuse to lose my body because one nipple is unfeeling, but I am willing to give up my whole wardrobe to make this point.

A Fire Without Light #342

The wind is a wall, and it never marks any territory for long. It will touch your blood to claim your blood. It will dazzle your soul as it changes your name. I don't think this man understands nature. I know he doesn't understand how a wall can turn on you at any moment.

A Fire Without Light #343

Now, all beauty is wild. There is no institutional beauty anymore. Meet me in the fields! We will eat the berries. We will place the flowers in our jackets. We will hang just enough tobacco to make victory cigars once we return from the capitol. We will bury our dead beneath the last beauty they remembered. We will return here every time we need to.

A Fire Without Light #344

I have walked around Ohio with dirt attached to my name. It turns out if you bathe in whiskey for a decade the ash will catch you right back. I have a small body, one the size of a quarter that hangs from my neck, that is silent all of the time because it's the body of my first son, the one that was never really born. I move slowly and quietly because I am called a good man despite the ash and body count that accompanies me, and because I am called a good man in whispers I walk without making a sound. Does this explain why Trump is so loud?

A Fire Without Light #352

Last night in Ohio they used pepper-spray on protesters. I suppose, taking in consideration what used to happen in Ohio when there were protests (Kent State), this was an improvement, but goddammit why were they in riot gear? There was no riot. There should have been a riot. There was no riot.

A Fire Without Light #353

Last night in Ohio they used pepper-spray on protesters. They did they expect the blood that was loosened to be gray and lifeless? They did they think that would dissipate the anger? They knew they had a chance to legally beat on people, and they took it. Fuck the police.

A Fire Without Light #354

Last night in Ohio they used pepper-spray on protesters. The rising was never yellow. It's not yellow now. We can survive a nation without light. We will be there, in the end, when the light returns to us like a wandering beast from the forest. Those of us in this have no exit strategy. We have our names. We have our families. We'll give up the rest if that's what it takes.

A Fire Without Light #383

We are going to have to name the dirt after the people we put in the dirt. How will we ever coax the fields again?

A Fire Without Light #415

The stars have opened their mouths to be indelicate against the black, to chant with the wagging tongue of the absence of heaven the same phrase in every language. There is no sleep in the cosmos. There is no retreat in the cosmos. When they chant "traitor" enough to change our weather patterns, then they have a message we should listen to.

A Fire Without Light #416

It's not cold enough to be winter. I can see everything he's doing. Still, this is a blizzard, and we are all in danger. I am driving my car on clean streets as if at any moment I could drive into the living room of a neighbor. I am listening to the storm. I am not listening for direction. I am singing in the wind. I am not safe. That part doesn't matter so much, but the muscles in my body thinks it is.

A Fire Without Light #419

I have wrapped my hand around the dark brick. I lift it every day. I am strong with a brick in my hand. That doesn't mean anything, but it feels good to know I can pick it up whenever I want to. It feels good to toss it up and down without swallowing any dust. It feels good to put it down gently, slow enough to tax my forearms. I type so swiftly after all of that. I believe in every word I write with this dark brick perched next to me.

A Fire Without Light #420

There is a mother in every marrow, and that mother is bear. Is he anxious right now? There are too many bodies full of bears in this country. Each bear tears against the tide that threatens each body. The moon remains unchallenged. He is not the moon.

A Fire Without Light #424

I see a king as light as a feather held on to by the teeth of wolves. The wind does nothing to him. The spittle is his joy. He is held so tightly by their sharp attention that it must at certain panicking points feel like real love meant to make his struggle valiant. He is a real man. That is his blood. If it's not his blood, then this story is really fucking dark

A Fire Without Light #425

The secrecy isn't cruel. The secrecy is a misplaced mercy. We have written down the names of so many people that would prefer us to be dead or at least gone. We have chanted some of those names. The secrecy is an animal without bones. It's useless, but it's important if we're going keep the fear that gives us these names.

A Fire Without Light #433

This fire sharpens box corners. These boxes cannot be stacked without a body count. I am still counting bodies. It would easier if I just stopped counting, but I'm not willing to give up that oxygen for nothing. This fire wants my oxygen. If I thought I could slow it down I would lay my oxygen as a present and a distraction, but that would only give a small jump to this fire. Unfettered consumption and the willingness to lie about what is consumed, that is their entire agenda. I will not be a part of that agenda. I'm writing down all of the names. I'm listing everything I lose. If we still have insurance companies when he is all done, I will present to them all five thousand of these poems.

A Fire Without Light #434

Faint copper, still working its way through the Ohio countryside, giving a glisten to each county line, I appreciate what it is you think you're doing, but we don't want to be shiny right now. That will only catch his gaze, and even though our evil governor hates this evil president he cannot stop him from trying to fit us inside his small fists.

A Fire Without Light #435

The apocalypse isn't coming. We're going to have to deal with all of this. An ending would be too easy. We are owed the whole of this process. We will have to carry him the same way we carried the rest of our original sins. How uncomfortable he will be riding America's back right next to the corpses of so many native, enslaved, and marginalized peoples. Great horrorman, meet the rest of our horrors, and speak to them about the American choice. We are lazy and evil, yet we sing almost all of the time. We have fired so many bullets into the heart of beauty because we thought gun smoke was the same thing as an early morning fog.

A Fire Without Light #440

I have been carving his face in butter. I make cakes when the sugar-ration allows me to. I dream of pies, but the act of holding can get you marked by his dark followers as a chaser of the light. I worship the crust of my family. We stay inside whenever we aren't marching against the taste of his terrible tide.

A Fire Without Light #441

The curtains are not bodies, but we love them like bodies. We close them as we open our dreams. We see the faces we need to see. We are disconnected from the carnage. It is selfish of us, but it's keeping us alive and in love with what it means to be alive. If we have that, then we can be the fists we need to be the rest of the time.

A Fire Without Light #463

Skin-built and bullied by the middle of the middle of the night, I have gone fishing for the full warmth of the bloom and I have been left with a sharp hook in my darkest time. That hook has become a friend of mine. I have danced with that hook. I have shorted out my television with that hook. I have hidden that hook on my body during the daytime. I am cut and cutting all of the time now. I have only one scar because I have no intention of bleeding more than I need to. I stand in the middle of my living room five times a day to rename that hook. I don't know what I'm doing, but it's enough of a distraction from the idea that I was intended to be the bloom. It's enough of a distraction from my country declaration that there are no blooms, and there never have been blooms. That hook is almost my whole world now.

A Fire Without Light #465

Do not consider the frayed rope. Consider the weight plummeting into the sea. If you can catch the whole world, then you can explain to me why we ever hung it off a cliff like an ornament. I swear, if you show me the torn threads of the original plan, I will scream at you for the rest of this gravity.

A Fire Without Light #471

I don't think he wants me to touch him. I'm going to touch him. I'm going to feel him, poorly. I'm to grasp and tug and pull. I'm going to ragdoll his body. I'm going to drag it casually through Zanesville, Ohio, and order a pizza for it. I'm going to buy drugs at the same pizza shop. I'm going talk to him for a long time about what it means to be preach into the mirrors of the world. I'm going to leave him in a mirror. I'm going to let him talk until he says a name other than his own. When he says my name I will put the rest of the pizza in the fridge of a stranger. I will let him keep the weed. I think he needs to get stoned on something other than our suffering.

A Fire Without Light #493

He is convinced we need a great storm. All I see is a hundred downed trees, and a distinct absence of song. Because every nest is fragile, we dare not kneel to anyone within our own spit and comfort.

A Fire Without Light #495

This is the same Ohio it's always been. We're a project. We're Jesus and a prayer. We've never really taken responsibility for anything. I can't talk anyone in my family into admitting that they can run without the wind of God. I think it's all so lovely when there are celebrations, but the rest of the time these people are too damn weak to do much about anything.

A Fire Without Light #503

It was a strange and compelling trick, but we (all of us) know now that this smoky field is America's faintest heartbeat. We know there is zero charm in the evisceration of our masterwork. Our deepest self is worth saving. I don't know what this fuck this is.

A Fire Without Light #511

All fathers are oil gifting oil.

A Fire Without Light #542

I've been thinking a lot about how the first tree was turned into something other than the first tree. Was it shelter? Was it a clue for fire? How many trees came from that first sapling? I've been thinking a lot of how that tree might have died, wasted as a curiosity, wasted as the individual before the forest, wasted on the animals that pissed around it. I have been thinking about how much animal piss is in my front yard. Even the deer have started to mark our oak tree. If a warthog arrives in my yard to yellow any of my plants, I will kill it. I will display it. I will send bad bacon to the president. He will take that as a threat, and I won't have entirely meant it that way.

A Fire Without Light #543

The light flares and I'm awake to the shadows overcoming Ohio. There is so much wasted stillness here. I love Ohio the same way I used to love cheap beer and fireworks and women that hated me; there's a puzzle piece rightness to the fit for me. That doesn't mean Ohio is the worst place. It just means the default setting for Ohio is fucking horrible. Ohio can change. I changed. I am still an awful man, but I make other decisions every single time now. Ohio could do that. Ohio will get the same offer I did before I quit drinking. Consumption works both ways, motherfucker, and everything in this world can be burnt into ash if it doesn't avoid the flammables. So, what you gonna do? Ohio, what you gonna do?

A Fire Without Light #545

Everywhere is the distinction between the air and air supply. I have already been called kindling. That is the language fire knows. That is the language fire breeds. Once again we are all searching for the water's edge. That's fine. Stick your heels in the pool. Turn to the flames. Move with the tide. Become the time. Keep breathing. Let the fear drown behind you.

A Fire Without Light #622

It's the evolution of the broken bottle. Once the glass is detached from its factory form it must cut to stay alive. He is a constant threat because he cannot be held without asking for blood. He cannot keep a single ounce of joy on the lip of his sharpest tip.

A Fire Without Light #644

The black market has no paintings and no jewels and no human organs. The black market has all of the truth. The truth and a hundred thousand kidnapped girls being sold into sex slavery. Do you think if we told Trump about the girls he might stumble into some actual truth before his purchases were finalized?

A Fire Without Light #645

Oh lovely bath tiles, thank you for holding me so often during these last few months. I am not done crying, but I need to make it to my computer so that I can shift my anger in front of this grief for the next eight hours. I can write poetry for eight hours today. I will return to pick at your grout when I can. My wife wants me to try and make dinner tonight.

A Fire Without Light #655

How lucky I am to be greeted with the wind as I smack back against the ribs of America. This is the era of bruising. Those of us that survive will look like survivors. Those of us that are buried will be buried in numerous plots. This is the shredding of the tendons of the American hopefuls. I have no intention of leaving. I have no idea if I can hold on to my country.

A Fire Without Light #672

I've been keeping hard candy in my fists. I cannot imagine yet in which way I will use the candy, or which way I will use my fists. I want most of all to buy my children's love with the sugar stuck to my open palm, but I don't think I'll be allowed to do that once I start throwing punches at the establishment. My children will lick my hands as the children of other animals lick their parent's bodies, and they will get all they can from before they leave me behind. If I do this right they will consume what they need from me before those that first forced my body to crumple in the middle of the Ohio kick me into the creek bed.

A Fire Without Light #702

Fuck the plums you've painted white. We don't want them. We want fruit that came from a tree that found a way to grow amidst no other trees. We want to be messy and righteous in that mess. We want the garden to make no sense at all. We want you out of the garden. You can shout at us from a very expensive distance. That is my final offer.

Acknowledgements

Anti-heroin Chic - #13, #14, #15
The Bees Are Dead - #86
Birds Piled Loosely - #101, #102
Black Market Review - #105
Bond Street Review - #30
CircleShow - #644, #645
Clemnentine Unbound - #172, #173, #174
Construction - #3, #4, #5
Contemporary American Voices - #672
Convergence #244, #245. #246
Creativity Webzine - #542, #543
Damfino - #113
The Electronic Pamphlet - #106, #108
Evening Street #252
Fire Poetry - #419, #420, #655
Five-Two Magazine - #226
Futures Trading - #35, #36
GloMag - #352, #353, #354
Killjoy - #109, #110, #111
Mad Swirl - #193
Mascara Review - #340, #341, #342
Nixes Mate - #493, #495
Northern New England Review - #45

Otis Nebula – #52, #463, #465
pacificReview – #383
poeticdiversity – #325
Poetry Superhighway – #22, #23, #24
Puerto del Sol – #415, #416
Quail Bell Magazine – #40, #41, #42
Randomly Accessed Poetics – #424, #425
Rasputin – #433, #434, #435
Rising Phoenix – #440, #441
Rogue Agent – #140
The Stay Project – #622
Stay Weird and Keep Writing – #76, #77, #78
Stickman Review – #471
Thirteen Myna Birds – #545
TL;DR – #127, #128, #129
Tuck Magazine – #115, #116, #117
Us for President – #122
Warscapes – #343, #344
Window Cat Press – #66
Wraparound South – #503
Your One Phone Call – #511

About the Author

Darren C. Demaree is from Mount Vernon, Ohio. He is a graduate of The College of Wooster and Miami University. He is the recipient of The Louis Bogan Award from Trio House Press and The Nancy Dew Taylor Prize from Emrys Journal. Outside of his own poetry, Darren is the founding editor of Ovenbird Poetry, as well the Managing Editor of the Best of the Net Anthology. Currently, he is enrolled in Kent State University's M.L.I.S. program, and is living and writing in Columbus, Ohio, with his wife and children. *A Fire Without Light* is his seventh collection of poetry.

Nixes Mate Books features small-batch artisanal literature, created by writers that use all 26 letters of the alphabet and then some, honing their craft the time-honored way: one line at a time.

Other or Forthcoming Nixes Mate titles:

WE ARE PROCESSION, SEISMOGRAPH | Devon Balwit
ON BROAD SOUND | Rusty Barnes
JESUS IN THE GHOST ROOM | Rusty Barnes
CAPP ROAD | Matt Borczon
HE WAS A GOOD FATHER | Mark Borczon
THE WILLOW HOWL | Lisa Brognano
A WORLD WHERE | Paul Brookes
SHE NEEDS THAT EDGE | Paul Brookes
SQUALL LINE ON THE HORIZON | Pris Campbell
MY SOUTHERN CHILDHOOD | Pris Campbell
LABOR | Lisa DeSiro
KINKY KEEPS THE HOUSE CLEAN | Mari Deweese
AIR & OTHER STORIES| Lauren Leja
HITCHHIKING BEATITUDES | Michael McInnis
SMOKEY OF THE MIGRAINES | Michael McInnis
THE LIVES OF ATOMS | Lee Okan
LUBBOCK ELECTRIC | Anne Elezabeth Pluto
STARLAND | Jessica Purdy
WAITING FOR AN ANSWER | Heather Sullivan
COMES TO THIS | Jeff Weddle
HEART OF THE BROKEN WORLD | Jeff Weddle
NIXES MATE REVIEW ANTHOLOGY 2016/17

nixesmate.pub/books

www.ingramcontent.com/pod-product-compliance
Lightning Source LLC
Chambersburg PA
CBHW052135010526
44113CB00036B/2267